BOOK 2

Popular Christmas Memories

MELODY BOBER

9 Intermediate Piano Arrangements of the Season's Most Popular Songs

When I think of Christmas, I am reminded of so many happy memories. These include a visit to grandma's, an extremely tall and beautiful Christmas tree, brightly wrapped presents, homemade goodies, and, of course, family sing-a-longs.

While sacred carols give the reason for the season, secular songs celebrate holiday delights such as newly fallen snow ("Suzy Snowflake"), a sleigh ride ("Jingle Bells"), or a visit from Santa Claus ("Believe," "Up on the Housetop," "Santa Claus is Comin' to Town"). A song can share the spirit of the season ("We Wish You a Merry Christmas," "The Twelve Days of Christmas") or provide a more nostalgic reflection ("I'll Be Home for Christmas"). And some songs are just plain fun ("Jingle Bell Rock")!

In *Popular Christmas Memories,* Book 2, I have arranged some of my favorite Christmas songs. It is my hope that your special Christmas memories will be rekindled during the holiday season through the pieces in this collection.

Merry Christmas!

Believe (from *The Polar Express*) 12

I'll Be Home for Christmas 22

Jingle Bell Rock 4

Jingle Bells. 19

Santa Claus Is Comin' to Town 10

Suzy Snowflake. 14

The Twelve Days of Christmas 16

Up on the Housetop 2

We Wish You a Merry Christmas. 7

Alfred

Copyright © MMIX by Alfred Music
All Rights Reserved

ISBN-10: 0-7390-6394-4
ISBN-13: 978-0-7390-6394-1

Up on the Housetop

Words and Music by Benjamin R. Hanby
Arr. by Melody Bober

Jingle Bell Rock

Words and Music by
Joe Beal and Jim Boothe
Arr. by Melody Bober

2nd time to Coda

We Wish You a Merry Christmas

Traditional English Carol
Arr. by Melody Bober

Santa Claus Is Comin' to Town

Words by Haven Gillespie
Music by J. Fred Coots
Arr. by Melody Bober

Believe
(from "*The Polar Express*")

Words and Music by
Alan Silvestri and Glenn Ballard
Arr. by Melody Bober

Suzy Snowflake

Words and Music by
Sid Tepper and Roy C. Bennett
Arr. by Melody Bober

The Twelve Days of Christmas

Traditional English Carol
Arr. by Melody Bober

Jingle Bells

Words and Music by James Pierpont
Arr. by Melody Bober

I'll Be Home for Christmas

Words by Kim Gannon
Music by Walter Kent
Arr. by Melody Bober